Looking - a collection

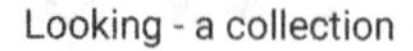

Table of Contents

Foreward

Choose your own adventure - You ever see those paperbacks in the library when you were in grade school? Was going to name one of the poems after those books. I did not but still enjoy the picture of someone hopping into this book and choosing the title from the table of contents which speaks to them most like a choose your own adventure.

The writings offered to the reader here are in the vein of the Audre Lorde essay 'Uses of the Erotic --- The Erotic As Power' and trying to achieve the emotional connectedness with another while seeing oneself through the existential concept of the Look. Also, in a couple of the notes and poems, confronting the affects of past traumas that still affect behaviors and hiding One's hurt from your Other to control how they see you i.e. not your problem, Showing (Each Other), In Dreams, et al..

There are alot of great poems here that honestly express erotic passion and the Look. The energy involved in creating these was enough to make the author mad but I managed to put this work together, even feel proud to have done so. If You want to ease into the erotic madness read from the back of the book. Be like foreplay that changes perspective before the fire. Or, jump in the fire and read it as arranged. I am critical of my concept poem 'Cryptonesia' but hope you get it. Regardless there are things in this book that have never been written and it is a privilege to bring them to You.

*capitalizing You, especially when writing "You and I" is done here to express equality in parties.

DISCLAIMER

The content within these pages may induce psychosis.
You will likely come, cry, and go crazy. On average the psychosis lasts about three days
but may vary from reader to reader. This exercise in madness will strengthen you after it
breaks you.
If you are experiencing difficulty with recovery please seek professional help from a
psychologist or support group (not a psychiatrist. psychiatrists perpetuate
pathologization).

That which is done with love always becomes beyond good and evil.

- - -Beyond Good and Evil
Frederick Wilhelm Nietzsche

The Spark (how it starts)

Those Eyes
feeling your spark
your measure
wonder what you are seeing
the movie in your mind
Do you believe?

Your power
to manifest
Be the Director
make your movie real
we can be stars
can fall hard
can fall slow
lift you up
manifest truth
Beyond Beyond
Those Eyes
feeling your spark
this is how it starts

falling hard
pressing in
pulling back
impact
making room
pressing beyond
against your wall
pain and pleasure
beyond
finding the way
blasting into depth
pulling rhythm building
freeing your cries
stacked and building
testify

those eyes
feeling your spark
this is how it starts

falling slow
riding my hand
open the gates
flood
ready
pressure steady
to your wall
move
beyond
press
and pull
press
beyond
hand by your ear
drunk on your scent
worried Look on your face
moans vibrate into me
feel you washing me
your flood
your love
Looking deep
those Eyes
feeling your spark
this is how it starts

Showing

feel me beat my drum
do I have your attention
desire to be seen

show your waterfall
power and force such treasure
wash me in your love

Insecure Narcissus

Looking for the Look
placing value
on how he's seen
giving pleasure
is getting pleasure
serving you
is serving himself
see me
feel me
love me
How to love myself
Loving you

hold me
set me free
from the abyss
ghosts that haunt
the memory
holding me

but don't say forever
cause when you see me
outside the flood
sorrows hard truth
trapdoor falls
down and alone
alone again
and every time
find a caring heart
waiting for the trapdoor
to drop

Narcissus Supremo

if you don't want me
please just watch me
with her
never seen a man so pink
Rose Pink and my pink toes
love the Look she gives
best thing she's ever seen
show her all of my tricks
work so hard to give you this
know you'll never forget
make it mystic
pull the stars from the sky
ecstatic waves of pleasure crashing into the sea
together
we are everything

Beyond The Look

What would you do
light a candle
try something new
Look to connect
beyond the shallows
in the river
of shared experience
not for you
nor for me
We

MAKING ROOM

first one is for me
give it all to you
hip to hip
against your wall
I move
all of me
feeling you
draw me out
life anew
first one is for me
all for you

Flight

see
we are brand new
day loving
the truth
let's go and hide
just want to be
with you
with you

show you my secret place
under the canopy
my favorite tree
the little things
softest flower
for you to feel
see
smell
and taste
you
drink from the stream
pure
all of me
all to you
seeing you
loving me
loving you
and what's to be
the secret place
give it all to you

Earth is for Lovers
 and here we are

Mercury

mind moving fast
engine pumping heat
I am mercury
closest to the sun
warm
Looking for the one
pull me from the sky
to You I come
drown this heat
in your sea
in your sea
rocking waves
rhythm of the night
waking with day
feel what You feel
feel what I feel
this heaven is yours
You are mine
I am thine
move fast through the sky
burning
waiting to find
this fall
to You
I rise
take this heat
into your sea
release

she said forever

my ex came over
told me the things about her boyfriend
that brought her to me
talked me into getting stoned
for a moment I forgot
smiled
she almost jumped onto me wrapping her arms around
to get ahold of me
finally finding her way through my hurt
her victory

we played with the cam site
but lost interest when the model answered my question
"no gemini i cannot see you and your girlfriend my cam is the only feed"
spent two hours making love to her
then she went home
with her revenge
her victory

Cryptonesia

hiding
carrying fear
but we
attracted to honesty
Looking in the eye
this is me
I see thee
feel
honestly
see you
creating
uniting
within
connect
connect
spark
spark
so much better
honestly
honestly
touch
charged
charged
power
full
exchange
making
love
love
honestly
free from fears
when you see me
Looking in the eye
this is me

this is thee
unite
honestly
connect
fear falls away
surrender
to connection
consent
honestly
free
creating
a line
spark
building
unite
honestly
honestly

mamas boy looking for the look

That little wyrm, little mamas boy, learned to value himself being seen in a woman's eyes so he is always conscious of all the Looks he receives. Learned his comfort comes being judged and held. Little wyrm is grown up still needing a woman's look or the value of his existence is unmeasured and he is unfulfilled. Still wants that comfort of being held. Still wants to be judged cause the more She sees the more of him is Hers. That little wyrm. Finding his value in being valued. Showing all he can do and be for Her. When he shows everything inside his messy heart there is the fear he is not valued and if he does not get validation that little wyrm just runs away and tortures himself by not being seen, not being valued, nonentity. That's not even the worst of it. When he finally finds someone who takes all of him he waits for the hurt cause the people who told him "I love you" as he was a toddler taught him trauma a few years later and beyond. So he looks for the look then either hides from it or waits for it to hurt him.

this is thee
unite
honestly
connect
fear falls away
surrender
to connection
consent
honestly
free
creating
a line
spark
building
unite
honestly
honestly

mamas boy looking for the look

That little wyrm, little mamas boy, learned to value himself being seen in a woman's eyes so he is always conscious of all the Looks he receives. Learned his comfort comes being judged and held. Little wyrm is grown up still needing a woman's look or the value of his existence is unmeasured and he is unfulfilled. Still wants that comfort of being held. Still wants to be judged cause the more She sees the more of him is Hers. That little wyrm. Finding his value in being valued. Showing all he can do and be for Her. When he shows everything inside his messy heart there is the fear he is not valued and if he does not get validation that little wyrm just runs away and tortures himself by not being seen, not being valued, nonentity. That's not even the worst of it. When he finally finds someone who takes all of him he waits for the hurt cause the people who told him "I love you" as he was a toddler taught him trauma a few years later and beyond. So he looks for the look then either hides from it or waits for it to hurt him.

Beyond the If

beyond the if
walk past the train
if it stops getting better
if you don't feel
if you turn away
when it stops getting better
if you will not say
one word long to hear
one word brings me near
sweetest sound
sets me free
Yes

beyond the if
past the train
seen the future
You make dreams
come true
beyond the if
step off the platform
into the dream
say the word
longing to hear
say the word
into the dream

beyond fears
beyond the if
to be
to become
inside you
make me feel
make me believe
in us in our love
step into your dream and
You make me
real

earth is for lovers
and here we are
tell me your dream

Salmon Leaps From Still Water

Walk with me to the river
feeling under the tree
rolling flow birdsong
ease into the rhythm
bring into the light
take me to your river
make everything right
You
make everything right

Pathologization (disclaimer supplement)

patient: doc, I'm sad.

psychiatrist: We call that clinical depression. Let me write you a prescription. There is this new drug. Company rep dropped off some pens and stationary pads. Want one?

Two years later...

patient: Doc, I'm still sad.

psychiatrist: If I was honest I would tell you that taking pills thinking it will make your life better does that to people. But, I just got back from a conference in San Diego which a pharmaceutical company paid for. They have this new product. Why don't we give it a try?

Pathologization (disclaimer supplement)

patient: doc, I'm sad.

psychiatrist: We call that clinical depression. Let me write you a prescription. There is this new drug. Company rep dropped off some pens and stationary pads. Want one?

Two years later...

patient: Doc, I'm still sad.

psychiatrist: If I was honest I would tell you that taking pills thinking it will make your life better does that to people. But, I just got back from a conference in San Diego which a pharmaceutical company paid for. They have this new product. Why don't we give it a try?

Possessing Touch

hands move
this touch to You
is mine
possessing feel
touch I give to You
feel what you feel
You make me real

You make me real
this touch I give
is mine and
I am Thine
surrendered to You
feel what You feel
You make me

Your current takes me
deep
river washes me
freed
surrender to you
feel what you feel
possessing touch
You are mine
I am Thine

earth is for lovers
and here we are

Romance Novel Stuff

romance novel sex
with the Look the Spark
eye contact drunk on each Others scent
feel our heartbeat inside
beyond close
beyond bounds
together
fate is Love
Love this fate
Love We Make
see me demand my gaze
see your beautiful face as waves of pleasure crash
crush
feeling you feeling me
free to release
making closer
believe

earth is for lovers
and here we are

Young Looks

In eighth grade I got in trouble for trying to sell one of my 20mg Dexedrine twelve hour release amphetamine capsules for fifty cents so I could buy a soda. After that I got in trouble for hitting a seventeen year old while wearing brass knuckles (only gave him a bloody lip. I was thirteen). The State dropped the assault charge and I pled to the drug charge. This started a string of incarcerations in Cowlitz County Juvenile Detention Center for pissing dirty for cannabis, runaway, or truency. The County Judge would sentence me to thirty days in juvey for each probation violation.

Messed up from earlier childhood traumas, I could not connect with anyone and did not have anyone to connect with. How can someone talk to their parents when those parents have attacked the child before and seek control by projecting anger on the child? Nice as an abuser is on any given day, you still know that abuser you are looking at carries hostility that could erupt anytime. So any dynamic where someone held more power than myself I had to avoid. After first being introduced to drugs by an abuser at nine years old, as a teen I got high in solitude. This worked to keep me away from any dynamic or connection and numbed the stress response that was always right behind my eyes ready to make me a crying mess. But I had to pay for my escape and the County made sure I did, in hard cells, overseen by people whose occupation is to hold children captive.

Did a lot of time on twenty-three and one hour restriction where I was only allowed out of the cell for one hour a day. Inside this "detention center", an opportunity the County wasted in what could have been an experience that nurtures psychological growth, learning how to address traumas that put something in the way of the child's ability to communicate, and developing healthy social connections, investing the good taxpayers money this way, the County instead invested in severe surfaces and locking the child, and others like him, into a dark cell with a book and a Bible.

When I was on twenty-three and one I would get my one hour walk at the same time that the girls pod across the hall ran the walk for the girls on twenty-three and one. There was this beautiful girl with big eyes, bright skin, and curls. Richly blended European-Greek-African. We would both get on the phone at the front glass of the pod with no one to call. Looking across the hallway into each others eyes. Two tortured kids trying to connect projecting our young heart's beat.

Christina, is her name, she was my friend Brett's girlfriend when they were teenagers after Christina and I were sharing Looks. When we were all twenty one-ish Brett was staying at my house and Christina came to stay for a bit. He sucked at being her man and left her for a crack mama who kept him high to keep him around (and ruined him). Think Christina moved to Reno to be a dancer.

When Christina stayed at the house with Brett, he tried to project anger at Christina as a lever to have power over her. But it did not work cause I was right there and the charge of energy which Christina and I had built as kids remained, reminding her how she is seen, guarding her. Something no one else shared. The Enduring Energy of Young Looks from two tortured kids trying to connect.

Nuestra Senora de la Rayo Divino

Feeling despondant, Our Lady sought refuge in the meadow. She sat under the sky and watched the swallows frolicking, dipping and shifting in aeronautic maneuvers. One of the birds landed on a juvenile Larch very near Our Lady. She looked at the smartly feathered male and spoke to him.

"It must be nice to be a bird. Taking to flight. Freeing yourself from this earth."

The bird looked at her beak agape. Our Lady understood wholely. There and then Our Lady resolved to surpass the heights of any human using the means granted to her by way of the being in whose image she was created to become.

change into a bird
make the flight others could not
return your eyes shine

=+=

The Lorde Prayer

come now patron saint of poets
keep this boy in your bosom
this new tool
no mercy for his sorrow
he must learn to carry this weight
but keep him from death
look after this boy
there when he fell to the earth
rebirth
kept him from death
as this tool took shape

come now patron saint of poets
as we come together
beyond difference
with influence
the tools
the master lacks
dismantle the force
based with
base beings
in costume

come now patron saint of poets
and guide me to the mother
bring you back
Pilar
heaven to earth
the ubermensch
She
will be

with these tools
the master lacks

build our world
for Her
for She

Patron saint of poets
tell us how our difference
makes us strong
Patron saint of poets
show them the power of connection
Patron saint of poets
be with us now
as we find the way

Patron saint of poets
the universe without and within
your words are still moving
divine sparks
brightening who we are
Patron saint of poets
you are with us
Lorde

Zones

places to put my face
sharing my touch
to make you feel
my love
feeling you
experiencing you
freed
nurturing the spark
growing
together
unlocking the power
your feeling
connection
under your ear
my lips
feeling your charge
tickled by your soft hair
as you flow unto me
feeling me
feeling you
freed
with you with me
freed
pleasures spark
friction
touch
more than biologic
metaphysic
appreciate You in ways
no one has before
for I am yours
and You gave me the chance
to love
share this spark
feel your treasure

You are treasured
and I am thine
give You forever
my lips under your ear
fingertips feeling
sharing
places I put my face
zones
love all of You
praise You
thank You
put me in the zone
your zones
feeling your spark
feeling our heart
beat
harder
seeing You
seeing Me
freed
we release
holding You close
safe
in the places
where I
put my face
zones

Your Narcissus Is Showing

plant yourself
on my root
thought you'd show me
laughter shakes my heart
hold your hips
show you
looking up to heaven
shake the rain from your clouds
I see God seeing your pleasured face
feel God in the spark we share
flood raining down
I am fulfilled
when you see me
feel me
tell me
with your cries freed
one two three
clouds emptied
how you see me
love
feel me
show me
who I am

your legs shake
you tell me
never been better
say to you
it only gets better
love to be your best
let me get you some water
know you are sore but..
we can make love better again
when you see me
feel me

tell me
moans vibrating
show me
who I am

Not Your Problem

Been holding back
so you don't see me
As just the hurt
the need

Cause what if
seeing
 you leave
Its not what
I wanted to be

Am I controlling
the way you see
not sharing
this hurt

you could know me
I am more
than what was done
and what its doing to me

Been holding back
trying to be
what you want
Cause I am more
than the need

Hiding
Controlling
how I am seen
but being seen
is what I need
But what if
what if
You see
too much

and not enough
the need and how
never have been enough
for someone
not to leave
So I've been hiding
trying to be
what you want
cause I am more
than the need

Good Morning

waking
next to you
your smell
your warmth
first thing I see
smile touches my eyes
desire my loins
reach
hand to your hip
down
lift your leg
pressure into you
lips on your neck
warm scent nosing your hair
you moan
vibrating
I move
Waking
in heaven
with you
with you
we move
we moan
washing me
waking me
your love
our love
we move
together
forever
better
we move
your love

our love
waking
inside
wrapping me
feeling you feeling me release
never want to wake without you
Always want to make
Love
our love
Good Morning

bring you coffee
and when you get up
you tell me what you call it
running down your leg
the Good Morning drip

Eros

Tell me who I am
Tonight
Touch bringing cosmic passion
elevating experience
feeling
spirit
engine pumping electric fire
universal movement
connecting with You
Tell me who I am
Show me how you feel
this too
Feeling
who we are
Becoming
Together
Its the Look we share
Showing who we are
Together
Becoming
Sharing
The Look
Elevating Experience
Cosmic touch
Passion
Pumping electric fire
Sharing
The Look
Becoming
Together
Showing
Who we are
Together
Together

The Dreamer

been dreaming
of making your dreams come true
been feeling
all your truth
knowing
it must be You
it must be You
was Looking
now your Look is what I need
fulfilled
with you with me
been feeling
and this is something new
heart is beating
to be with You
been dreaming
of making your dreams come true
fresh flowers
big shiny stone
lightning your eye
our eyes
babe in our arms
make a house a home
was Looking
now I see
You are all I will
my need

Been dreaming
of waking next to You
feeling
knowing
this truth
heart beats
to be with You

Fati Amor

walk right in right on time
just what I hoped to find
scan the room till you see
first Look eyes meet change of mien
feeling you feel it too
don't need a drink
let's talk about this deja vu

do you dream the future too
know its weird to know
but what can we do
this is me this is you
fati amor
dreams come true
amor fati
sharing truth
this is me this is you
fati amor
you with me me with you
fati amor and deja vu

Her Starry Crown

I was the sky
until She brought me to Earth
to ride
plant herself upon me
lean back taking her time
Her beauty taking me
Her feeling finding
making me
like a rope pulling me
deep desire thrusting into Her sea
She unlocked everything
making me
Hers
everything I want to be
in Her
She is my sky
satisfied
Her pleasured face
tells me everything
is alright
releasing me
pleasured cries washing me
Her starry crown
Lighting
in Her eyes
I am freed

Showing (Each Other)

There is this couple. Each of them has survived childhood abuses and later survived
abusive relationships. Looking for someone who wanted more than to possess,
manipulate, and control, they sought someone whom they could share an emotional
connection and eventually found each other. There is a Damocles Sword for the abused
and they have this inescapable feeling that the good is too good to be true, waiting for
the trapdoor to drop them into the hurt. Each of them faced this sense of impending
hurt and betrayal, which was put upon them by those abusers who had taught them a
false image of love. Each of the lovers suffer the returning feeling that they were not
seen as who they truly are and then believing to love is to hurt and accepting the hurt as
deserving. These Saints found each other and lived with this sense of coming hurt,
betrayal, but faced it together and shared with each other everyday who they truly are.
Showing each other what real love Looks like and it is to be seen in each others eyes,
finding their smiling face, the loving intent of their actions. Showing, in an arms race of
Loving acts making each other rich in Love. Showing each Other.

Firefighter

Summer lingers
Wilderness waits for Rain
come with me
under the canopy
will set your river free
save me from my fire
with Your waters of Love
One word longing to hear

Come with me under the canopy
see this wild garden grow
smell these bright flowers
feel this thorn
see You in my wild garden
brightest bloom of all

meet this fire with your river
save me make me feel
while trees wait for rain
fearing the spark
save them save me
set your river free

Thorny

Face To Face Sharing
The Look
Pleasures Pain
Fulfilling Penetration
Touch
Together
Our Heartbeat One
Fulfilling
One Being
Becoming
Better
Moving Together
Coming Together
Sharing
The Spark

Excerpt from 'Kashoki and Scotia's Magi - an Evergreen Sickness Book 1 - (a novel - coming soon)

Spreading in a pocket of a small valley between two foothills of the Andes Mountains outside of Lima, Peru, the seminary campus included Spanish colonial era buildings built with the labor of the subjugated Peruvian Peoples overseen by the Jesuits on their mission to bring their kingdom of heaven to earth. Johnny's daily task was to ride a motorscooter carrying a basket of bread on his back to the trailhead, then carry the basket of bread on his back another two miles to the Peoples village. The basket had bright purple and yellow cloth carrying straps which dug into the flesh of Johnny's shoulders when he returned from the village loaded with potatoes or the fruits which the People sent to the Church.

The hairy and happy Monsignor Rivas, an enologist, was joyed to apprentice Johnny in the craft of cultivating yeast to harvest the byproduct, which was wine. Rivas called it "Working the First Miracle" and demystified the science while instructing Johnny on the importance of the sacrament. Rivas gave a history of the grape, explained zymurgy (cultivating and studying yeasts), and how yeast, this one celled animal-like fungus, drove mankind to a better understanding of biology. Making Johnny memorize the history and and learn the names of Fabroni, Lavoisier, Roscoe, Helmholtz, Monsier Appert, Hugo Von Mohl: their respective discoveries and how those discoveries helped lead mankind in its measurements of the Universe. That was how Johnny learned to work the First Miracle. Or in other words: how to turn water into wine.

Eleven days into his occupation stepping onto the worn trail carrying the bread basket to the People. Flora hiding Johnny and a whole world away from the sky. Came a strike to Johnny's brow. He tottered but kept his footing as a cacophony of howls and shaking branches erupted from the canopy above his bleeding head. Blood flowed into his right eye and dripped onto his monk costume and the cloth strip of the bread basket. Looking up he saw the assailant's eyes meet his own as the monkey stretched his neck and pushed the resonant call from his body.

Johnny, wounded and seething with impotent rage made his way to the village. Pondering how and why the beast attacked him. "Maybe I was too quiet and surprised him.", "Perhaps he was protecting his harem of lady monkeys.", but the thought of the beast watching Johnny approach to ambush him and revel in schadenfreude and the expression of the beast's own power was the thought in the current of Johnny's neural pathways as he left the world under the canopy and entered the clearing of the village.

He was met by Yesenia, the Chief's wife, who met Johnny for every delivery and exchange of cargo if there was any. She was alarmed at the young man's bloody appearance and had him explain what had happened before she led Johnny to her husband, Chief David. Yesenia told her Husband how Johnny, the bringer of bread, had been ambushed by a beast most foul who has broken the peace with the People. Johnny admired her artful embellishments and animation and shared a look with Chief David whose mein held the amused look of enjoyment at beholding his beloved communicate this happening.

Johnny found himself a player in a dance of village life. Chief David declared that the peace must be restored and "Un Mano Malo debe morir.". Chief David directed Johnny to remove his seminary costume. Standing in his grey boxer briefs Johnny was told by Chief David he must be able to move freely and walked away leaving Johnny standing in his underwear as the village began to gather to look over and measure the wound and the pale and pink teenage body before them.

Chief David returned with three of his men and armed Johnny with a bow and arrows. At a log behind one of the homes a leaf was pasted to the log using mud. Getting over feeling the energy of the Look of the People by following Chief David's instructions to breath and let it flow, Johnny hit the leaf with the third arrow. Emotionally connected and present Johnny had visualized the mechanics of the bow into a oneness with his will and focused his will to move the arrow. Making several hits on target until the leaf was gone and only a mark from the mud and gouged arrow marks remained. Chief David was satisfied the People had witnessed how he had transformed Johnny the bringer of bread into a bowman.

Chief David pointed a finger and mimicked the flight of an arrow pressing it into Johnny's chest.
"Corrazone."
"Si. Corrazone." Johnny answered.

Chief David and his men trailed behind Johnny as he led the way to the place of the ambush. As he approached the place Johnny held up a fist like he had seen in a war movie about jungle warfare in southeast Asia. Johnny pointed to the spot El Mono Malo had been. Chief David pointed at Johnny, then his own heart, and then gave the hand signal that looks like a chop but means onward and Johnny approached alone.

The pounding of his heart was so intense he could feel blood pumping to his scalp and believed everyone present, including the forest, could feel the thunderous drum beat of his engine. Creeping in the shadows of the canopy with the bow drawn. Alerted by Johnny's heart or having smelt the iron of Johnny's blood El Mono Malo howled. Johnny had his target. The shot was true.

His heart's pounding in his ears he did not hear the men approach gathering around gripping Johnny's shoulders and patting his back in camaraderie Looking into Johnny's eyes with warmth and joy, to witness his becoming as he watched El Mono Malo.

Chief David spoke.
"Todo aqui solo mentes."
Then motioned for Johnny to retrieve the monkey.

El Mono Malo had haltingly tried to climb away from the wound and failed in his attempts to hold onto the tree, his body failing him as the blood escaped, ending fallen and motionless at the base of the tree from the death Johnny and the People had willed for El Mono Malo. Johnny ran his hand on the sorrel coat and shifted the head so he could look at the face. The face gave Johnny the impression of being thoughtful in death. He pictured a divine light receiving the monkey's spirit. The more Johnny examined the monkey he saw more color. Seeing the coat as closer to ginger than sorrel and peppered with grey on the shoulders, back, even the hands. Seeing the thick sharp nails on the hands and feet. The hands were at least twice larger than the feet but similar in structure. Large brown ears at the crown instead of the center of the head as humans have. The hair on his crown was thicker and softer than the rest.

"Adios, El Mono Malo." Johnny spoke as he ran his hand through the soft fur of the crown.

Pablo, one of the Chief's men, tied the arms and feet together with cords he had brought for this purpose. The monkey was placed on Johnny same as a backpack or the breadbasket. The body was warm against his naked back. They returned to the village, Johnny walking with the meat backpack tail bouncing off his legs as he walked.

Juan took the monkey to the water to be butchered and fired. Yesenia led Johnny to an open long house with four supporting posts but no walls and sat him on a bench at a long table. She served him a bowl of the People's wine. It had the pure alcohol smell like vodka. He drank the whole bowl fearing a bite from a bad taste which would make him gag and lose face but the drink went down as smooth as water. Chills tickled up his spine and shook his shoulders. The Chief's daughter Maria arrived with a cloth and small pot of hot water to wash the wound on Johnny's brow. Yesenia served him another bowl of wine.

Maria was near Johnny's age if not slightly older. The perfect example of her People. She sat the pot on the table, put one leg over the bench where Johnny sat, standing near and over him as she washed his face and hands. He was enraptured in her dark eyes. Warmed by the wine. His mouth dry. She met his Look and put her hand on his shoulder. He felt her charge.

Monsignor Rivas showed up at the village the following morning. Johnny had been worrying and expected the Monsignor to come for him. This foreknowledge made Johnny mindful enough to put his monk's garb on and kiss Maria when he heard the dogs bark, then go rushing to meet Rivas before he could discover Johnny and Maria in their marital bed.

Rivas looked him over measuringly noticing the cut. Johnny told Rivas all about the monkey and the moonlight feast, omitting the marriage ceremony, the dance, and any detail of how he and Maria had spent the night. Chief David came to greet Rivas and expressed his affection for Johnny saying in his heart he is one of the people.
"We are all of the body of Christ." Rivas countered.

Rivas appeared suspicious. Johnny appeared nervous. Rivas asked if there was any problem with Johnny. Chief David answered.
"No, no problmo, padre. El Primero Hombre. Aqui bienvenido siempre."
Chief David gave a warm smile and put his hand on the back of Johnny's neck. Looking Johnny in the eye with an honest familial love.

The trip back to the seminary Johnny had to push the motor scooter for the entirety of the trip to keep pace with Rivas. Suspecting it was out of penance because his offer to ride on the back as Rivas drove the scooter was dismissed. Legs and shoulders aching, answering Rivas' questions telling of El Mono Malo's ambush, the cut (minus Maria cleaning the wound and possessing him by meeting his Look and with the touch on his shoulder), the kill, and the meal that went into the night. Johnny did not lie about drinking and was ordered to do five Our Father and five Hail Mary prayers. Upon return to the seminary Johnny still had to fulfill his duty and bring the People their daily bread.

Everyday Johnny brought the bread to the village and stayed with Maria in the hut which the people had constructed for the couple to share. Maria had her own door to enter and leave from and Johnny had his own door on the opposite wall. This house was solely their place where the magic of their sacred meeting lived. The place for their spirit.

When the rains came the humidity made sweat leak from every pore of Johnny's body. His thoughts were torturous reflecting the physical misery brought by the climate telling him his time of bliss with Maria was coming to an end. He poured himself out to her, taught her English and sang to her. Placing his hand on the swell of her womb. He sang 'Loch Lomond', the song his Grandparents used to play with Grandmother on the fiddle Grandfather on the accordion. Johnny wept knowing he would be leaving her and the Leader of the people they had manifested together like they were writing the future with their words in the place where the magic of their coming together lived.

As he wept Maria's gaze turned hot and the tone of her speech burned him as she told him the history of how one of the men had attacked her the year before and violated her until her scream brought help. Chief David and Pablo beat the man and struck him with a large stick, but the man escaped. Chief David paid men from town to slay the man who had violated Maria because the people do not kill men as in the times before they became Christian. Johnny wept hearing how she hurt and the fire within her. The forcefulness of her sharing affected Johnny. Heat from the charge their magic he was betraying. The weight of leaving her and their child alone, abandoning their love, their magic. Maria watched his face as the heat of her words rendered his spirit and made him understand what abandoning her made him.

Years later, in the abyss of solitary confinement where magnified reflection was his only company, Johnny meditated on his time in the jungle with Maria, her love, the perfect love of the People, and the heart piercing regret of turning away and not fighting with every fiber of his being to be there and experience what the People and Maria had given him. In times of perpetual misfortune knowing it was his due for not having returned. A curse.

Drinking and Laughing
Drinking and Crying
Sadness comes and goes
But we are still here
Life Between the Dreams
Dance and Dance Some More
It is a joy to be held

Not All Looks Are Created Equal

In the Valley
 in the houses marked by discordance
 in the night the exhaust of trading damage for an artificial light
 a high
raising strange clouds over the city
 while the good people dream
while the good people dream

[story not valuing Looks and the revenge of the spurned censored due to content]

[portion censored for content] probably would have had a better chance just starting a conversation and pursuing a connection with me instead of [censored for content] and trying to get me into a transactional situation [portion censored for content]. Or, from an approach of appealing to the biological instinct to mate (if I was just an animal) would have had a better shot [censored]. I am not a hungry baby so [censored for content] are not much use to me. They are fun to cuddle and look upon but the approach was all wrong for the target audience. I was not in the mood. Living in the slow suicide of addiction to keep occupied, hiding from the grief and childhood traumas which affected me, following the path of personal destruction. Being broken and miserable made me use sharp comments to project my hurt and despondency on others who reached for me. My bad. Ever get 'Vindicated' to be a thing I will give some overdue apologies for my sharp comments and rejections. "I would give you a ride but unfortunately my car does not run on friendship and happy thoughts...", etc..

There were alot of women that probably would have been good for me (previously mentioned excluded) which I should have fallen into their love, but I was not being good to myself and had an occupation of needful pain that got in the way of anything worth having and doing. I had not done the work to make myself worth loving. In magnified reflections pouring over my past life while I have been in solitary confinement (aprx. 8 years total) I have thought about every time I turned a woman down where I should have pursued instead of pushing that connection away. That one at the trap house is not one which I regret pushing away, no matter how cruel that individual was.

I want to feel safe like a baby monkey cuddling mama. With a great woman who lets me know it is safe so I feel free to show and express my appreciation for sharing her love with me. Open to be seen and loved by someone worth loving. Someone impressive I

can connect to emotionally and intellectually and we can come together to find the way to create and manifest greatness. Smertle. What I do not want is to be subjected to some Id driven abuser's need to project control.
see also demisexual

In Summation:

°Not all Looks are created equal.

°Meth monsters are not safe.

°I'm a cuddler.

°Ladies, if you find a broken mamas boy worth having, the key is to make him feel safe and pursue an emotional connection by getting him to talk about all the shit that has broken him and See him and love him beyond that and you win your broken mamas boy.

°And Lastly, 'Vindicated' needs to be a show on Amazon, but only choice content that can humanize the liars enough to give them a chance to admit their misdeed and it can be analysed by the consumer. Not any Jerry Springer bullshit. It is about the pursuit of truth, vindication, psychological growth, and resolving past traumas especially those wrought by deceit.

Treasured

The most beautiful stone
deep in the earth
unmeasured
Light never has touched
awaken thee
sparkle glimmer and shine
held within
to be Seen
measured

this treasure
unknown
and
unmeasured
How it could light your eyes
sparkle your breast
being seen
compliment
your glory
color your life

Where are today's treasure hunters?
Where is your treasure?
seek ye first
nay not the superficial
filters and control
to achieve
biological function
There is more to this Life

Seek ye first
treasure
worth seeking
seek ye first
connection worth having

There is a treasure
within
buried, waiting to be discovered
wanting to be expressed
pouring itself out
making many rich
Seek ye first
dig down and wash this dirt
from the undiscovered stone
Let the Light come through
sparkle your eyes and shine

Where are the treasure hunters?
Where is the seeker?
Find these
Find the Way
Seek ye first
Find the Way
Most treasured on this Earth
Seekers
Unlocking the treasure within
Finding the Way
Where is your Treasure?

In Dreams

Found the place where
 I can be happy
in your dreams
where I am free
you see me
 happy

burned the bar down
spent all my money
to forget
but the darkness
always hits again

You find the place
to hide me
see me happy
tell me
how you see me
in dreams

Lost in the spoon
wake up
meet the needful pain
slip away
but the hurt returns
and things just get worse

Can't leave it behind
hits everyday
sometimes I leave
freed
from gravity
like the way you see

in your dream
sometimes life is
bright
and everything is great
could not ask for more
moving
Becoming
Fulfilling
meeting
but I see
the sadness
behind every beautiful thing
Can live with this
when you sleep
and you hold me
In Dreams

merrily merrily sorrowful
all around the mulberry bush
or gently down the stream
hide myself where I can be happy
In Dreams
In Dreams

Hide and Seek

no
called to attend her ache
made it like a game
showed the boy how to heal
with touch
then wanted too much
it was always too much
touch

bring a tool to reach the ache
tell him how to touch
with your high power toy
three times
wanting too much
lower lower
lower
had to push away
run away
try to find the boy
hide and seek

call the costumes
men with guns
who hunt the boy
hide and seek
captured then locked away
until the day
arrive
with gifts
Guarding
Controlling
Chasing his friends away
girls that saw him as a treasure
threaten control

of how he was seen
how he saw himself
run away
hide and seek
so high he couldn't speak
escaping

hiding
hiding so long
he hid from himself
all he could be
finding someone
but She couldn't reach
needed tools to breach
doors where he locked away
the pain
the betrayal
the shame
unexpressed without measure
in darkness
abyss stealing his time
forestalls connection
Something in the way

In the night
In the drink
without words
sometimes it showed
tears and madness
unmeasured
without the words to express

In the days
In the spoon
occupied with anesthesia
needful pain
launching rocks
into his own river
drowning

beating himself on the rocks
no happy endings
undeserving
unmeasured
waiting expectant
to meet his end

So here you are
been expecting you
dreamed about this
months ago
Saw this
Looking out on a prison yard

Looking for a crack
The one
Where the Light gets in
Finding the words
Carpenter's tools
breaching the Doors
wind rushing
into his darkest hiding place
speaking the words
expression purging
covering the abyss
with a white sheet
to bring
Growth Healing Restoration
Fulfillment
She gives to him
what was taken
Power
agency
choice
to be
to become
Fulfilled
Know

Dames and Dolphins

Two thousand four had a dream of standing in front of a thirty gallon fishtank and there were two little dolphins inside swimming clockwise before breaking the circle of their path to Look at me with this open energy of love. Two thousand twenty two, three of the best British Women left their existence in human form. I was affected by not having these magnificent Women among us in human form any longer. Twenty twenty three, my friend had this drawing from her her ex. This ex who had went on a campaign of murder threats against her as well as enlisting the aid of about a dozen people (incarcerated and free) to send threats and harassment to her and her daughters (two years prior this ex had betrayed me also but that is another story). The ex had drawn and sent her this drawing which he did out of his compulsion to express his power over someone I treasured. It was a drawing of Dame Olivia Newton-John portrayed as a demon. Using this drawing of the Dame Olivia, who I love, portrayed as a demonic fallen being (which She never was and never could be She is so good) to focus his energy and intent. So I had been begging my friend to burn this demonic garbage as a burnt offering to make the Universe better and She does. Same evening We were on the phone talking and She remarks how much I adore Dame O.N.J. and I am speaking about how Dame O.N.J. had this spiritual connection to the dolphins. My friend checks my network page for me, and I follow Joy Harjo cause She is also great and a poet and one of Audre Lorde's disciples and I just love her, so me and my friend are speaking about the dolphins and Joy posts a funny little thing about dolphin language finally being translated and it is all cuss words directed toward humans. But it was a moment. That night I remembered my dream from two thousand four and I finally knew what it meant. Things were coming full circle. Like the little dolphins in the fishtank swimming in the circle.

Your burnt offering
and the poet hears the dolphins sing
dancing under the moon
fly above the sea
only want to be your friend
swim with me and see
Your burnt offering

and the dolphins sang
see them dancing in the starlight
hear them sing love to you
feel the love in the Look they share
feel the love

Great Blue Heron

stepping through the swamp
master of her world
on the hunt
finding the frog to feed her chick
master of her world
her shadow passes over
spirit of the swamp
covered me briefly
with me always
with me always

another crazy bird
master of my world
hunted by men with wicked designs
in spite of all opposition
master of my world

in spite of all opposition
She is
She is
She is
master of Her world

Never Ending

Good does not end
It lives on even in
The Ashes

A Spark
waiting to be stirred
bring the breath
Air

Waiting
to rise with you
within

The Spark
lighting your eyes
lighting your life
warming
Those you bring near

You carry the fire
this is your gift
You carry the fire
even in the ashes
You carry the fire

The Lovers

Know those hundred year old Lovers? It is not that one dies then the other sees no reason to stay and dies of a broken heart. It is that the first Lover went before to prepare their path in the afterworld.

Calling Me to You
You show me
Things brand new
Open to me
Things I never knew
You make Me
New

It is You
It is You

Earth is for Lovers
There We Were

Love Lives On
Calling Me to You

Grateful

Everything
feel your heartbeat when I see You
feel the miracle of your love
everyday you blessed
everyday making this world better
give me everything
without you ask myself
what I would give
to get you back
everything
what do I have
with You with Me
Everything

SURRENDER

would worship you
whatever you want
that's what I'll do

She puts her feet on me
feel safe cause I am
where She is
look down from above
seeing how I am seen
She is everything
sets me free

lay in the Arcadian afterglow
falling rain of small daisy flowers with pink tipped petals
She fingers the scars
no words
there is honesty in the tears
She kisses
give her a squeeze
and surrender
to her
the hurt
the hurt
letting go
surrender control
her tears healing me
She has her territory
She is the Sun
Her rain cleanses
Her river draws me out
She is the Sun
Her light on this broken land
sprouts new grasses covering

once a quiet waste
filled with the laughter of flowers

She is the answer
Always was
Fati Amor

Among the wet green grasses
small daisy flowers
petals pink tipped
bruised by the cold of night
meeting the Sun
meeting the Sun
Fati Amor

Earth is for Lovers
Fati Amor
Laughter of the Flowers
blooms erupt ahead
to meet you on
your right path
Earth is for Lovers

Thorn

Not here to break you
when you let me make you
Feel my command
these pretty thorns
move and mark
hold and pull
See You Feel
will not break you

trust my command
firm hold steady
hair in my hand
head back
Looking at me
Feel my hand
move you
how you want to feel
white hot shock
print pink vibrating electricity
feeling me
possessing my touch
we share
this heat
this light
day and night

not going to break you
lay you down
open
Pressure
bury myself in you
surrendered unto me
this pretty thorn

moves with You
pressure beyond
to your wall
Trust my command
Fulfill
these Passion's demand

In plentitude of power
I want your revenge
cause You won't break me
when You make me
Feel
want you above me
with me
buried deep
make me feel
your pretty thorns
your flowers garden
madness in Love
Eros
Show me and know me
how I want you
to move
make me feel

know you make me
will not break me
Make You Feel
my Love

Going Down

go down to your river to pray
don't come up for air
till you come
Riding my face
can't breath
could die happy
Live for You
masked
wearing you

Give the same to You
show me
know me
make me feel
You make me
real

You make me feel
You make me real

Virile

In Plentitude of Power
Statuesque
One word post Yes
More
Make your dreams reality
Foot atop your enemy
Queen of Light
We ride

We came and Became
More
Their measure was off
This Joker up your sleeve, Thee
Game is yours
In Plentitude of Power
Statuesque
One Word Post Yes
More

Earth is for Lovers
And Here We Are
Own the World Always Home

Smertle (sch-'mur-toll) n the frequency of doing stuff and thinking things at the highest possible level.
see also existentialist see also enlightenment

Crier's Abuses

from their high places
they call you down
demanding you submit
acknowledge the illusion of
their projected power
this movie screen is a mirror
nails pointing out
when your abuse does not affect
never will submit
never will accept
your power is an illusion
and I am real

only power something has
is what it is given
will never give power away
in spite of all opposition
I am still here
I am still here
abuser cannot bring me down
cry "Burn The Witch!"
from your high place
looks like a sewer to me

told you not to touch me
shatter your illusion
reflecting unto you
the truth
told you to leave
told you no
you attack
now you run
run run

run

and I am still here
the criers cry, "Burn the Witch! Burn the Witch!"
In spite of all opposition
I am still here
shining
shining

they are still there
crying lies
and I am still here
I am still here

Misc.

Being Queen means never saying sorry.

If you are Looking for trouble...I am Looking for a husband/wife.

Ever had your abuser tell you to stop feeling sorry for yourself?

Break of Betrayal

It could be feeling the breaking of the Look, could be breaking the Erotic Emotional
Connection, or it could be what St. Paul wrote about the flesh becoming one and feeling
that bond broken. That feeling when your Other sleeps with someone else and you
know. Feel it in every cell of your being. That drop through the trap door. Maybe its
different for you but I remember the feel of that connection breaking as I stood alone
under the sky on that crisp starry night. Then the Look on my Other's face knowing that
I knew.

Capitalism In Relationships

If they choose someone else..it is my fault for not convincing them I am the best. If they
lie it is my fault for not showing them I deserve the truth. Making them SEE. Asking
what more can I do to show them? But I did show them and I am better than who they
chose to mess around with, then come back to me. To them it was not about having the
best and sharing an unbroken connection. To them it was about power. They used that
power to show they could break that connection. Show they had more power than the
best they ever had.

Victim's Blaming

"Everything is my fault...". Knowing One is not to blame for being the victim of an attack,
again, and again, but blaming One's self for everything else.

"It is my fault they betrayed our relationship, broke that connection. I never surrendered my hurt and my thoughts to them. They needed power and had to find it hurting me. It is my fault."

Miserable P.O.S.

Abusers project control over others and look for any lever they can find to gain control (something you care about, fear, violence, relief/comfort, drugs). see also Leverage In Abusive Relationships

Residual Trauma

Thought about this concept of Residual Trauma where those who witness the aftermath of attacks and have to examine the events, or, those who treat the victims, are affected by being exposed to the victim's pain, effects of the depravity of the abuser/attacker. (emergency room nurses and doctors, see also the courtroom where lawyers and judges examine sexual assaults, violence, and murders). These people carry that residue in their head home at the end of their workday.

Thoughts For Any Season (and concepts)

One in four women have been the victim of sexual assault. This number is as high as eight out of ten in some regions/countries. For every woman who experiences violence She experiences 100% of the attack and is 100% affected by it. These attacks are crimes against humanity achieving the greatest manifestation of existence which still waits to Become with Her.

Society is broken if this is acceptable. The State "justice" system which handles over ninety nine percent of sex offenses coddles sex offenders giving light sentences and allows the abuser/attacker to plea down sex offenses to lower ranked felony offenses. The Patriarchal construction which has allowed the Court to conduct itself this way sends the message to abusers/attackers that sexual assault is excusable and that the victim who suffers sexual violence is not recognized.

SHE IS THE UBERMENSCH (bringer of new values)

Imagine civics courses for all young women. That the Patriarchy was overturned and women were the exclusive holders of public office. No more men aping behind a podium projecting their power through wars. Instead Woman's nurturing and intuitiveness in the high places of power. This is the concept of Messianic Feminism. It works for more than the macro level of government, but in the individual level where connection and being seen and valued in Her Look saves a man from the disease of self contempt.

HER Bushido Coupled With Chivalry

In feudal era Japan ladies carried daggers to defend themselves. Today a lovely piece of metal would be a stylish accessory to an ensemble evidencing an assault would be cost prohibitive. T'would be sexist to dismiss a lady carrying a weapon as unbecoming. Our young ladies should know they are the most sought after treasure on this earth, that the churls are out to steal and destroy her, and learned to be responsible with this metal claw (how to shift gears in an attacker's groin). Also, our young ladies are studying civics, economics, contemporary global politics, Audre Lorde and other existentialist philosophical thought in order to take their place as community leaders when they reach the proper age for civic service, which is minimum forty years old (seventy five should be the age limit, it is awful paying the salaries of public officials to watch them hold power as they lose their cognitive function, bumbling through their days selling us out to weapons makers and corporate interests obligating our nations children to go fight in wars and granting subsidies to bad products the market does not support).

Couple this matriarchal governance with raising our boys and men to hold the noble virtues sacred and that they are the standard bearers for their queen. Also that it is a man's duty to be impressive (what you do is what you are - if you have done nothing, you are not) so that She will choose him to build Her nest and allow him the privilege of making this earth more like heaven for Her. Respecting and honoring women, knowing it is the greatest honor to be chosen and gifted with the opportunity to show Her how good he is, being the best he can be, being the best father and friend, showing he deserves to be valued by Her. Also when all our government leaders are women the earth will be a place where the men will have more time to do man stuff like woodworking and fishing.

Manifesting this vision of community requires coming together and that individuals stop practicing the Id driven abusive method which projects power through force to establish a dominance hierarchy over others. Instead we have leaders with the capacity to articulate their vision and do not rely on political tribalism and corporate funded ad saturation to gain positional power.

None of this is said to victim blame, but to express a vision of new values where women receive respect and are cherished for creating the future. Without HER there is no future. What we have now is not working for any of us. We need a direction and it is with Her. Happy wife, happy life... Stop clipping her wings and they will not just cover us, they will carry us.

How I Met Audre Lorde and Why Her Essays Are a Necessity Today

How I Met Audre Lorde

The first time I met Audre Lorde was in twenty nineteen when I was stuck in Washington Correction Center. I was there after I had seen my words move in men's hearts and minds at Clallam Bay Correction Center and how the spark grew and broke the State in three days with a prison work and hunger strike (there were a few low minded individuals that suffer from Stockholm Syndrome and a few other low minded individuals that gave in before the three days, the latter I believe out of their own psychological defects that lead them to reach for control. I digress). My involvement in this endeavor ended after laying the foundation, providing the blueprint, and writing the list of demands. Regardless the struggle continued to get the State to back away from many of the unjustly applied practices and exercises of power that are inevitable in the Captor/Captive Power Dynamic. See also Stanford Prison Experiment (SPE) Haney, Zimbardo, Hanson 1973.

I was placed in IMU (solitary confinement), not because of any revolutionary work, but because some lame ran up as many drug debts as he could and checked into protective custody with the meth inspired plan to get to a lower custody level by telling the State all of his meth inspired stories of how the author was the shot caller and doing all kinds of gangster stuff (I was going to college classes, the only opportunity the State ever provided me to do so in the ten years I had been in prison at that time, was also doing the extra curricular activity of providing input and engineering the prisoner work and hunger strike, oh and also cultivating yeast to harvest the byproduct so I could dance with myself and listen to Sirius xm and feel so good I wonder if the songs on Prime Country were part of my serendipitous fate. see also Amor Fati). So I got thrown in IMU with this shot caller write up that projects this image of me being a small time Barry Mills. I request witness statements from everyone whose name I can think of and some guys around the State whose prisoner numbers I have in my address book. I even get the best witness statement from the guy who was allegedly targeted for assault, which the lame who checked in to Protective Custody had owed money to.

 The strike happens. The State acquiesces to some of the demands. My favorite was to start making the lunch meals at Clallam Bay to serve Clallam Bay instead of having the lunch trays assembled at Airway Heights (a special needs/sex offender prison on the other side of the State, which shipping the meals from was creating a needless expense and enlarging the State's carbon footprint), it also brought jobs for prisoners to Clallam Bay which is a good thing. One of the demands was supposed to be changing the mail restriction on nudity but the "hardened prisoners" who spoke to the administration to negotiate the strike settlement were too bashful to make the request. I could have a Rubens on my wall right now if those clowns had a pair.

The day of the settlement the State does a special chain bus to get the most influential men out of that prison and even though I am in IMU (solitary confinement) awaiting my Hearing for the shot caller accusations the State sends me to the IMU at Washington Correction Center to have the disciplinary hearing. After a month in this hole awaiting the State to gather all the witness statements I requested (real rainbow coalition of support I put together with my ten witness statements and by this time I had been in solitary confinement about three months), the State finally does my Hearing and finds me not guilty of all charges. Kicked out of IMU that night I get sent to the receiving unit and get celled up with a twenty six year old ginger, who is also a Gemini, and I tell him, "Don't worry. Keep your bottom bunk. I should be out of here back to the Bay next chain.". We were cellys for three months.

Every time I was scheduled to leave some notable violence would occur at Clallam Bay and the chain bus would get canceled. (This violence was a symptom of the State destabilizing the population dynamics by taking all the smartest men out of the prison and an influx of new faces and the violent entropy is a direct consequence of the State's meddling and reaching for control same as an abuser does, instead of letting water find its level and operating the prison based on consent, connection, and a Psychological Growth Based Approach to the State's engineered prison experience). As terrible as it is living in a six by nine foot cell with another man for all but eight hours a week when we get our walks or the three showers we get each week, we sought and found the magic in our days and functioned at our highest possible levels and I got to teach my celly all sorts of tricks for being superior to the constrictions of the State's engineered Prison Experience, and alot about psychology, Prison Power Dynamics, chiropractic method and techniques, and how to have fun making the best of a bad situation my way. See also Smertle.

Books. Getting books was an occupation that demanded serious attention. New books and magazines are restricted mail for prisoners housed in receiving. Once a week the Prison would drop off a box of donated books at the gym in the lower receiving area where I was housed. But there are three units in lower receiving, so if this week my unit does not get first gym on book day the pickings are old timey religious books, grocery store fiction you would see at the checkout line at a grocery store or on a wire rack that can spin in a drug store, and ugly murder and crime books for low frequency thinkers with unexamined lives. Making social connections provided avenues to make many things happen while I was stuck in receiving with my ginger gemini sidekick and we did achieve the goal of our occupation to get the best books. 'Infinite Jest' by Scott Foster Wallace, 'The Wrath and the Wind', a poetry journal from Portland, Oregon, which hipped me to 'Blood Meridian' by Cormac McCarthy, and the Women's Studies book where I first met Saint Audre Lorde.

When I read 'Uses of the Erotic - - - The Erotic As Power' I found IT. I am a seeker. Looking for the divine spark to ride and ascend each day, the existential reason for being at every minute - at every place - in every interaction (is this going anywhere? and, what is the right word?).
The way Saint Audre framed the Erotic as being emotionally connected to your existence being contra to the superficial is such a profound tool for anyone to possess. I fell in love and became an evangelist for 'Uses of the Erotic - - - The Erotic As Power'.

Why Audre Lorde's Essays Are A Necessity Today

Have only seen Saint Audre's image one time and it was a flash for a PBS program about the feminist movement that aired in March 2022. How unappreciated Saint Audre's essays are makes me think of the song 'Vincent' by Don McLean. Audre is everything. She died of breast cancer in the same time as my childhood was going from awful to worse. Like when her flesh betrayed her and she died, the world experienced an entropy when it lost the physical body which contained all this creative energy giving it order and creating values. Her words remain reminding us of Her eye for picking the existential fight which called us to come together and be better.

'Uses of the Erotic - - - The Erotic As Power'

An Erotic Existence vs the Superficial. Saint Audre was so on with this concept. It is an existentialist tool and exactly what is needed today to address the nihilism that is cultivated by the industries who pimp superficiality and seek to please the lowest need of humans, the pleasure drive, the Id. An Erotic emotionally connected existence is contra to using the social media based lens to view one's self, contra to the consumer based value system where acquiring things and consumption is the pursuit of one's self, contra to pursuing control of how one is viewed by others based on superficial appearances (surgeries, drugs, consuming products and not pursuits in optimal wellness), contra to political tribalism and consuming the media products which promote low frequency thought to sell you insurance and laundry detergent at the commercial break.

In 'Uses of the Erotic - - - The Erotic As Power' Saint Audre was mining the same vein as Nietzsche did in 'Will To Power', but She got deeper cause she saw it through her unique perspective. When we see these mass shootings tearing apart lives and snuffing out the biological existence of God's Children we ask "Why?". Many point to the tool which was used and neglect to examine the psychology and what nurtured such a violent reaction. Those superficial distractions that lead one away from becoming take someone so deep into nonentity there is no sight of the way to become and one begins to believe this superficial pursuit was their search for meaning in life and after reaching the pinnacle of knowledge in the pursuit of this superficial path they find no purpose and reject life.

There is no answer to the question: " to what purpose?" [WTP 2]

"Nihilism" (the penetrating feeling of nonentity) [WTP 1020]

The logical denial of the world is a consequence of the fact that we must oppose
nonentity with Being, and that Becoming is denied. ("Something becomes.). [WTP 580]

The personal journey to discover one's self, become emotionally connected to all one
does, and Become. This is the Erotic As Power and the answer which will bankrupt the
industries whose products cultivate nihilism. 'Uses of the Erotic - - - The Erotic As
Power' is a necessity today and I wish that as a teen I had learned the tools the essay
contains for measuring one's existence and the world back then cause it would have
enriched my existence so much, especially classifying getting loaded as superficial and
not Erotic.

Audre's Erotic is Existential

The Master's Tools Will Never Dismantle Master's House

With this essay Saint Audre left a lot of meat on the bone for us future philosophers.
She could have done more with the truths She gave after she owned the "Master's
House" of academics who held the keys to the house and invited Audre to a conference
but did not invite Audre to engineer and help shape the conference (which would have
made it amazing, world creating. Instead the only name I know from that conference
today is Audre Lorde). Wanted to juxtaposition Audre's owning these academics and
their conference with Nietzsche's take down of Nineteenth Century Christendom in
Europe, but it is not that severe and more Audre claiming the power of command by
using her words to do a medicine dance where She spreads her wings and stretches
showing an impressive display of her feathers. After Saint Audre does her dance and
takes command of the conference She shows briefly what the conference could have
been had these academic gatekeepers not been focused on their order and control and
instead given Saint Audre the positional power to use her influence to nurture an open
space for the free flow of power and creativity where Saint Audre could have brought
her friends and owned the world. see also Aza Weir-Soley. see also Joy Harjo.

In the Norse creation myth, the opposing energies of Muspelhiem and Niflheim meet over the Void and this meeting of opposing energies gives rise to being. In Hebrew mythology God entered the darkness and said "Let there be light." again the meeting of opposing energies giving rise to being. This ancient truth was what Saint Audre brought to that academic conference: Our differences make us strong and provide us with the power to create if we come together. One of the "Master's Tool's" is dividing us from each other to keep us focused on what the Master points to. see also Political Tribalism. see also Media And The Effects On The Psyche. When we are focused on where the Master directs we fail to see our own agency to find the Way to achieve the greatest manifestation of our being. Meet others and aid in their becoming. The meeting of energies provides us with the strength to create a better world where we are our own masters.

The meat Audre left on the bone that I am getting after is identifying the Master's tools and sharpening our own. I had only read about this essay and had to wait a moon for it to be sent to me here in the hole the entire moon contemplating the title. With my measuring of the state engineered structure that I am a prisoner in I had developed the picture of Positional Power vs Influential Power being the focus of the essay with the freedom of Bohemianism being the body of the essay, but learned this is my own vision for dismantling the Master's house, although Audre did touch on coming together and our differences making us stronger she left alot of meat on the bone.

Beyond barring access to institutions, the Master's Tools of Positional Power utilize force, the gun, the "justice" system, the Prison Industrial Complex with its incapacitating levers of deprivation, degradation, and discomfort. Hold up the mirror to the Master, measure, and use tools that are not the Positional Power of "Or Else.". Our Power is contra Positional Power. Our Power is Influential Power. Our Power comes from Truth, Consent, and Connection. Not the lies and manipulation of Political Tribalism. Our Power is the Power the Master fears and would use every tool and lever to keep you from realizing: the Power of your own agency to utilize your influence.

Our Power can dismantle the Master's house.

POETRY IS NOT A LUXURY

SHE has been unexpressed and must seek the unexpressed deep within her which holds her power which has been locked away without celebration. This power locked within She has been taught to fear and feel shame for. So heavy. This same examination of ones inner most being that Saint Audre pointed to as the path to personal empowerment and poetry being a necessity and the way to power is what we use to address our trauma today. We measure it and make ourselves strong and keep measuring our trauma until through all this exercise we make ourselves bigger than our traumas and the effects that those past traumas have caused. (see also ECHOES - Something In the Way and Your River, Little Ways, 2023, Jeremiah Park). We must measure ourselves and all that we have locked away within our spirit, from undefined and unmeasured traumas that have put something in the way of one being emotionally connected to one's most valuable possession: existence, to unlocking the greatness that is within waiting to be discovered and manifest itself in your life. Being brought out by measuring, identifying, and pursuing that greatness. Just as a poet reaches for the word to define and transmit, One must reach for the greatness within to define and express their existence.

Seeing how woman has been portrayed as a mystery begs me to ask:

 Is it because the low frequency thought traffickers are incapable of understanding?

Is Woman projected as a mystery because examining what the Patriarchy has done to Women would be too labor intensive for the low frequency thinkers who value their worth in projecting power to subjugate others especially Women?

Where would the human race be if it pursued manifesting the nurturing and intuitive nature of Woman?

The human race has pursued every wicked whim of the male of the species to fruition, are we as a society going to continue to repeat these same patterns of consumption, subjugation, and destruction?

What would our world be when the Ubermensch is female and She brings the new values to mankind?

Let's see what Mama has for us. Wrap us and dress our wounds. Trust and honesty appeal more to this author than the apes with guns marching for the corporations who fund the men wearing suits in Washington and G20s transferring taxpayer wealth for their designs. ie. war, subjugation of the population, and planetary degradation for corporate profits.

In Summation:

° Need to put it on my project list to rework the Don McLean song 'Vincent', which told the story of Vincent Van Gogh's unappreciated beauty, to 'Audre' telling the story of how the world is missing out on the wisdom this existential revolutionary brought with Her cosmological creative energy.

° Need to get the number of the board member whom I will present all my concepts for shows and content to. see also 'Vindicated', 'The Divine Comedy' and 'Thus Spoke Sara Thustra' (Little Ways, 2023).

Excerpts from 'Human, All Too Human - a book for free spirits' F.W.N.

Part 1

377.

The Perfect Woman - The perfect woman is a higher type of humanity than the perfect man, and also something much rarer. The natural history of animals furnishes grounds in support of this theory.

384.

A Male Disease. - The surest remedy for the male disease of self contempt is to be loved by a sensible woman.

Part 2

95.

"Love." --- The finest artistic conception wherein Christianity had the advantage over other religious systems lay in one word - - - Love. Hence it became the lyric religion (whereas in its two other creations Semitism bestowed heroico-epical religions upon the world). In the word "love" there is so much meaning, so much that stimulates and appeals to memory and hope, that even the meanest intelligence and the coldest heart feel some glimmering of its sense. The cleverest woman and the lowest man think of the comparatively unselfish moments of their whole life, even if Eros never soared high: and the vast number of beings who miss love from their parents or children or sweethearts, especially those whose sexual instincts have been refined away, have found their heart's desire in Christianity.

274.

Man Promises, Woman Fulfills. - By woman Nature shows how far She has hitherto achieved Her task of fashioning humanity, by man She shows what She has had to overcome and what She still proposes to do for humanity. - The most perfect woman of every age is the joyful pleasure of the Creator on every seventh day of culture, the recreation of the artist from their work.

273.

Raising and Lowering in the Sexual Domain. --- The storm of desire will sometimes carry a man up to a height where all desire is silenced, where he really loves and lives in a better state of being rather than in a better state of choice. On the other hand, a good woman, from true love, often climbs down to desire, and lowers herself in her own eyes. The latter action in particular is one of the most pathetic sensations which the idea of a good marriage can involve.

H2H (2023)

If She is ever drawn from the path of Her ascending through pity Her name must be erased from the list of Ubermensch.
 - - - Thus Spoke Sara Thustra

Man promises, Woman fulfills.

Love Man Promises, Woman Fulfills Love

Woman Fulfills

MORE THOUGHTS FOR ANY SEASON

Plastic Surgery - These "Doctors" need to promote an image which individuals want to achieve. These "Doctors" will say what they need to to get an individual on the table to cut on them in order to put money in the "Doctor's" pocket. Creating and focusing an individual's attention on the image does forestall Becoming. The individual becomes a consumer seeking control of their image. Victim of the Patriarchy which shows individuals that they will not be seen if they do not have the attention of man because in this Patriarchal culture/society man has determined the value of woman for all of history and every measure is engineered to reflect this. Every institution and culture has held woman back so men could occupy the positions of power. Using the positional power of the Patriarchy to subjugate and victimize women. Keep HER from Becoming. see also 'Human, All Too Human' 274. Man Promises, Woman Fulfills. Nietzsche

Nietzsche + Lorde Walking

Imagine the thoughts they thought as they walked...

These existential warriors walking, explorers of existence penetrating powers and principalities. Conquering institutions by understanding where these institutions are deficient because these institutions stifle humanity's Becoming (Patriarchy, Race As A Measure / Historic Racial Barriers, Nineteenth century christendom making god in Man's image, etc.). These existential warriors thinking every thought, explorers of conscious existence seeking to be most aware. They left breadcrumbs for us future philosophers in their writings for us to get to the meat on the bone which still remains in the works they left for us. Those measurer's who found understanding makes One a conquerer left the breadcrumbs leading us future philosophers to the victory and fulfillment in manifesting the greatest self in each of us. Walking to the prize, writing to the future.

Patriarchy - There are anti trust laws which are used to break up monopolies. Something like one in four women are victims of sexual violence, as high as seven or eight out of ten in certain countries/regions. Time for a lever to break up the monopoly of the Patriarchy which has failed Her. The Patriarchy perpetuates the projecting of power over others to achieve dominion. This system of thought teaches the path to power is found in projecting force over others using levers to victimize and create a hierarchy. This system must be deconstructed and it cannot be deconstructed using the Master's tools of force. The dismantling must come from influence and consent. However, no quarter must be given to those forces which seek to stifle influence through violence and using force to silence this movement. Abusers must be called to account.

de facto Widowhood - A husband/Other does not have to be deceased for the Wife to become a de facto widow. Any action which makes the husband/Other unavailable to being present and connected is de facto Widowhood. i.e. If a man chooses drugs over the connection with his wife and duty to the family She does not have a husband. If a man chooses pornography over earning Her attention and affections She does not have a husband. If a man is abusive She is a widow because She does not have a husband She has an abuser.

The New Values - connection, consent, healthful expression, manifesting the greatest self for every individual needs to be the aim which She, the Ubermensch brings us.

mistress waits
another broken date
lonesome night
into the drink
into the dark
sound of tires
light from passing cars
reflects from wet pavement
puppy he brought to distract
 from the sorrow
of what he made her do

afternoon lunch
business like clockwork
waits to receive
his prepared words
to soothe her sorrow
but Mistress waits
another broken date
walk the dog
bag the mess
should have been a baby
rain comes down

another day
he brings a gift
how good I have been!
treat for the dog
what's wrong?
let me kiss it better
see?
no
no
its all wrong

arnt I good?

pay your rent
the dog
you're lucky
look at all I do for you
what more do you want?
come here
arnt I good to you
see that's nice

Mistress waits
nothing fills the empty space
every touch wounds
reminds
apartment a cage
kept
new coat jewelry money for food
arnt I good to you?
no
no

Looking - a collection

Acknowledgments

Pathologization - discovered this term/concept from Dr. Jessica Taylor. She is an intellectual giant with a mind moving fast, hot, powerful. She is right about everything, except I disagree with her discounting the ACEs measurement scale (Adverse Childhood Experiences). The ACEs is a tool which studies have shown those who experience childhood trauma are more likely to end up with negative life outcomes. Something like 80% of prisoners have an ACEs score of greater than four (the more types of trauma experienced as a child the greater the ACEs score, the scale tops out at ten). The ACEs may not measure the impacts of a specific traumatic event, but it is a useful measure which can be used in shifting the State's engineered prison experience from one of incapacitation and degradation to an engineered experience in psychological growth where the childhood traumas which put "Something In The Way" of an individual's development are addressed and focus is placed on cultivating the ability to find the way to being emotionally connected to existence, the individual learning to believe they are worth more than what was done to them, and that they have value to the community as they measure the effects of traumatic experience and learn to be bigger than those trauma's effects. Using the ACEs measurement scale is a valuable tool which should be used to identify the need of individuals who have not addressed the effects of childhood trauma and have negative life outcomes which reflect their being unfulfilled, in prison. The State should not be perpetuating the image of worthlessness through incapacitation. As the State operates now it takes in broken individuals and releases them more broken (if the State releases them at all).

de facto Widowhood - discovered this concept from the Betrayal Traumas Recovery podcast. Two days before sending this book to be packaged and submitted to Amazon, the following named episode was uploaded with Anne expounding upon the concept (though not named 'de facto Widowhood' by Anne): Betrayal Trauma Recovery, Clergy, Court Professionals, Counselors: Help, Dont [sic] Harm, Sept 26, 2023. Hope including this resource helps someone. Love the BTR podcast. Anne, the host, always has the best guests. I can identify with men being abusers and this is the podcast that introduced me to Dr. Jessica Taylor. When I first discovered this podcast I listened to three episodes and was paranoid of myself from my being a man.

The concept I encountered in BTR which spoke to me most was the idea of being emotionally unavailable as abuse (This relates to what Saint Audre Lorde expressed in Her essay 'Uses of the Erotic - - - The Erotic As Power'). I watched my Father's porn addiction lead him to being emotionally disconnected from my mother and us kids. He would go to his computer room and look at porn after work, then he sat in front of his computer looking and searching for porn for twenty some years. Porn addiction feeds the pleasure drive, the Id. The violence I experienced was a symptom of the Id being put in control and the Id's will to project control and exercise power over others. (Id, is the beast in the Id/Ego/Super-Ego psychic apparatus model which the Ego is rides upon seeking to mitigate the Id's projections of power/control to gain pleasure so as not to cause trouble - the Super-Ego is the conscience which aligns One to their highest values and sits above the Ego in the Id/Ego/Super-Ego model). The Id is the pleasure drive and this drive seeks to project control over others. The Id is characterized as the beast which the Ego rides upon.

I have studied abusers and learned to identify when individuals are abusers by their seeking to project power over others or looking for a lever to use to exercise power over others. Healthy individuals seek connection, not control. Emotional connection and consent is healthy. The BTR podcast is a good resource for those who wish to become informed of the levers abusers will use to manipulate others. See also how abusers seek to create a hierarchy and do not crave connection and equality but to project their will on others.

*Freud was a cocaine addict who was wrong about women in about every way probably because of what the coke he injected did to distort his thinking. What he did have which I found useful and sound is the Id/Ego/Super-Ego model.

Dame O.N.J. (Dames and Dolphins) - The poem included in 'Dames and Dolphins' is a continuation of Dame Olivia Newton-John's Dolphin Song inspired by the events written in the 'Dames and Dolphins' offering. The other two British Women mentioned in the offering who had left their existence in human form that year were Christine McVie and Queen Elizabeth.

If You want to hear how talented a singer is, watch and hear their ability to meet the moment in a live performance. Want to hear a pro meet the moment check out: Magic - Olivia Newton-John featuring The Sydney Orchestra

The author lived his non-captive life in the Cowlitz and Willamette Valleys. Prosecuted by the State for things he did and did not do. Regrets taking plea bargains to secure release from jail instead of pursuing the cases to trial. One of these cases occurred when the author had a reaction to drugs (amytriptaline and benzodiazapines) while trying to kick heroin back in 2005 and the author's girlfriend called the costumes when the author called her the wrong name (Pam, when her name is Kristin. "Why are you trying to break me and my girlfriend up Pam?") and the responding costume took the author to jail unresponsive, then the costume had to take the author to the hospital to be revived before taking the author back to the jail where the author awoke the next morning clueless what happened or why he was on a mat in a jail cell wearing a suicide smock. (the author and Kristin were very codependent and refused to be apart and the author ended up with three no contact order violations for the two's disregarding the State's Order to stay apart). Another conviction for not allowing his mother to take away his car keys. And two for fighting with his brother. Those are the ones the author should have taken to trial instead of taking a plea bargain to get released from starving in the Cowlitz County Jail and being separated from his sad slow suicide.

Author is currently awaiting a hearing for a Motion for a New Trial to address the discovery of undisclosed evidence of the State's witness tampering in the murder trial where the State achieved the conviction by using every lever at its disposal to elevate the testimony of a witness who was called in to give four written statements in three days time to create the "murder" case, and that witness' testimony was contrary to three other witnesses as well as being contrary to the written statements and the physical evidence. The State did not disclose evidence of directing costumes to contact the witness in the community to apply pressure and to having the witness jailed in Oregon to "Go over there and see how cooperative she is." "Get her in jail then we will have her pretty little body for trial." "Since we so urgently needed her arrested I had her P.O. put a rush on that warrant." [excerpts from the State's email exchanges documenting undisclosed witness tampering which denied the author the due process of a fair trial by forestalling author/defendant's ability to confront the witness.]. Months before the trial, the State also failed to disclose how the State conspired with the witness's probation officer in Oregon to have the witness kidnapped by Longview Police Officers to have the witness brought to Washington, the Longview Police Officers operating outside of the law in another State outside of their jurisdictional boundaries, but the good jailers refused to go along with the conspiracy to kidnap the witness and refused to hold her until the Longview Police arrived to kidnap her, releasing her instead.

Author has been held in solitary confinement since March 26, 2021, due to his exercising his right to remain silent in regard to the State's investigation into an attack on the author, who was not a bad guy, was unharmed in an attempted assault against his person, and shamed all involved with the ineffectual ambush.

Following the author's upcoming Court hearing and release from captivity, a production crew will document the author's reentry into the community and sinking into despondency while seeking to play tennis and only finding pickle ballers on all the tennis courts, as well as documenting the author's other pursuits (French Bulldog Uberhound breeding program, Old Growth Habitat Conservation, Eradicating invasive species from the Cowlitz valley + Columbia river, working with Cowlitz Tribal to create the Cowlitz Sporting Guild so kids in the Cowlitz valley have a safe place for growth and do not have to experience traumas while also cultivating the stewardship required to conserve the good parts of our planet for the future generations of flora and fauna, Starting a regional culture magazine, Messianic Feminism, Modern Bohemianism, Elder care that aims to keep seniors in their homes with their pets, Converting a historic hotel into an elder care facility: hotel folks home, Pitching at least one show to Amazon every week or so, Securing land for local food production/food security, Promoting health and wellness in the valley, and taking a professor emeritus job at one of the local colleges in one of the author's many areas of study ((Philosophy, Psychology, Injustice/ Law, Poetry, Literature, Fitness))).

Other Works By The Author

Kashoki and Scotia's Magi - a novel -

Little Ways - a collection -

Looking - a collection -

Finding The Way: Choosing Triumph Over Trauma

Coming Soon:

Entropy and Ennui - a novel -

Our Lady of the Divine Spark

Misclit

Mamas Boys: the girl who blew up the car

Knights of Magonia

9 798859 975921